PAST AND PRESENT

OF

ARMAMENTISM

ISBN: 9781688645226

PAST AND PRESENT

OF

ARMAMENTISM

Juan Sanz Sanz

Between August and September 1983, just now the whopping thirty-six years, JUAN SANZ SANZ (1943 - 2019), developed a thorough study to which he put the following title: PAST AND PRESENT OF ARMAMENTISM.

Unfortunately, the very cultured man has just passed away, a self-taught man who many would not hesitate to describe as a prototype of a person close to the Renaissance for the large amount of knowledge which throughout its existence tried to enlarge.

The baggage provided by his wisdom, due to the depth of the immersion he did for decades in Geography and History, together with the careful observation of how much was happening in those years throughout the Planet, then gave the author the necessary impulse to share his written reflections, privately and individually, to some of his contemporaries.

With unequal luck he was welcomed, PAST AND PRESENT OF ARMAMENTISM, and it is good remember again that we talked about 1983. From the most expressive congratulations that were made by very high-ranking people and, to the indifference and unauthorization of some of the recipients of the copies that he distributed, a whole panoply of reactions was triggered in which a word weighed heavily against him, una always present in a hierarchical excess society: self-taught

Without moving a comma from his legacy, his work is now published for the first time.

In memoriam

CHAPTERS:

STATE OF CRISIS

The feeling of crisis, that civilization is in danger, is not something new in the history of man. Sometimes because social conflicts seemed to have no solution, sometimes because threats from abroad were invincible and sometimes because of fateful dates that predicted the end of the world, throughout history we find numerous testimonies of it.

Our civilization lives with this feeling. It seems as if the future is not possible. The current man does not make long-term plans, does not look forward, trying to lay the foundations of what will be within a generation or a century. The future appears as something dark, blurred, whose profile we cannot define; We see it with suspicion and distrust. And all this, why? Because collective consciousness lives under the weight, under the threat that radioactive weapons mean for the survival of Humanity. Everyone is aware of it. From the layman to the initiate, they know what it means. It is a murky, threatening phenomenon, that is there, that clouds the full feeling of life, that closes the way forward. We are all aware of what a conflagration represents with this type of disproportionate, monstrous, unusual weapons.

Humanity lives uneasily with the strange sensation that any day may be the last, that the war that annihilates it could explode at any moment. It is like the incurable patient, who only lives in the present and makes no plans for the future. We are immersed in an anomalous situation, which occurs from late to late and that must be addressed and resolved. This is the big problem that man has before him. He needs to shake off this threat and live without the evil influence of this nightmare, to look safely at the future and make it possible with his work and his effort.

This is the great challenge of our time, the first that needs to be solved. Humanity feels helpless, on the edge of the abyss. As long as you do not overcome this obstacle, you cannot move on. If it does not solve it, it will be a victim of itself, of the destructive germs that society carries with it.

But in our time there are no external enemies who threaten civilization, since it extends throughout the planet and the societies that live there are governed by its principles; nor does it come from the apocalyptic omen of a fatal date. Nor are they social conflicts, which cause endless fratricidal and devastating struggles, which arouse this desperate feeling. This situation has been produced by the appearance in our century of a new and disturbing element - the knowledge of the process of the disintegration of matter - which first emerged as another step in the scientific process, but which has taken the form of one. of those destructive germs that civilization generates. The double effect of the excessive destructive power and the indelible radioactive contamination is the cause of this feeling of threat that goes not only against society, but also against all the life that dwells on our Planet.

It is such a serious fact, so absolute, that today's man has a great effort to face it. However, the fact is there, indisputable, irreversible, and you have to face it. Humanity has encountered other times in desperate and apocalyptic situations and has managed to overcome them. What we suffer now is, perhaps, the most external of all. The danger we face today is the greatest man has ever suffered since its appearance on the face of the Earth.

He has to overcome it, as he overcame the previous dangers. For this, it is necessary to face the problem clearly and without inhibitions, without the disgust produced by the analysis of this destructive phenomenon obstructing the intellect and preventing us from trying to solve it.

TROUBLES OF THE ROMAN REPUBLIC

In most cases, this sense of destructive threat, of irresistible danger, has been motivated by the pressure of peoples outside civilization. When society entered into crisis, its ability to defend itself weakened and added to the evils of social upheaval and internal confusion, the predatory effort of societies strangers to it. Until our time, all civilizations have developed in a limited geographical space. Only ours covers the entire planet, and this is a new situation, which poses new problems. But so far, there have always been around civilizations a vast swath of space inhabited by semi-wild peoples, of culture reflected only in the military terrain, which were set in motion as soon as the defensive tension of the culture loosened. Innovations in military technique are the first to be transmitted and that radiate further, and it is explainable because independence or slavery, survival or extermination often depend on its application. Putting things in this limit, it is natural that improvements in military technique have been avidly imitated by the people who were in contact with civilization and whose existence was much more unstable and violent.

As civilization periodically enters crisis, these movements towards the interior of the outer towns have been repeated in the same way. At every period of crisis, there has been another invasion or invasion attempt, which has sown terror and confusion in civilization, accentuating its evils. Throughout Greco-Roman history we can follow this process exactly.

When the conquests of Alexander emptied the Greek world to the East, the Celtic peoples that inhabited the Balkan peninsula devastated the Greek cities; the invasion of the Celts or Gauls proved irresistible to the more armies powerful of the world of that time. Later, in the period of fullness of the Roman Republic, but coinciding with the social crisis that begins with the Graces, the Germanic peoples are set in motion. The Mediterranean civilization was bound by a strip of European peoples, which was double. More wax, the Celts or Gauls; and to the north the Germanic peoples. The Celtic peoples threatened Greece and Italy in the third century but were gradually acculturated and ceased to be a danger. At the end of the second century, coinciding with the Roman social crisis, the Germanic peoples began a penetration, first on the Celtic strip and later in the territories of the old Mediterranean culture. These towns were barbarians, strangers to civilization, from which, however, they had adopted a good part of their military techniques. They were army-peoples, who lived from war. They toured Gaul in all directions and then entered Italy. Although their number as a people was not excessive, all the men were combatants and could gather on the battlefield some contingent's superior to those of the great Roman armies. They witnessed their depredations helplessly over the territories of their Gauls associates and waited with great fear for the moment when the invading surge will enter Italy. At the same time, in the South, the semi-wild Mogreb nummids carry out a similar action. It was a critical moment. The Roman Republic and, with it, the Mediterranean civilization, believed that its last hour arrived; but they knew how to react, finding solutions for such an arduous problem. Given the mass of contingents that were necessary to mobilize to deal with the double invasion, the structure of Roman society had to be completely modified. In the first place, the army ceased to be the privilege of the middle class, which provided its weapons to it and the spoils were distributed to that extent. Popular armies appear, equipped by the State, and recruited among the plebs, not only from the city of Rome, but from the other Italian cities. This fact would later produce great consequences. With the masses that were able to be recruited in this way, the Romans managed to shake off the Germanic and Berber threat, not without great troubles and over the years. From then on, Roman society would no longer be the same. These masses who had contributed decisively to overcome the danger, were aware of it and demanded their rights.

The social struggle, which had begun timidly at the time of the Graces, would intensify until it became a civil war, after which Roman society ceased to be a closed oligarchy, making possible coexistence within the ancient cities. A general agreement was reached between the social classes of the Mediterranean world, which would later take the form of the Roman Empire. It would be precisely César who shaped the new State and its policy was also determined by this invading phenomenon. Once the invasion was over, it was necessary to prevent it from now on. Cesar's action consisted of incorporating into society Mediterranean the Gallic peoples, partially acculturated and potential natural allies, to create in Gaul a nucleus of resistance against new Germanic invasions. With this, the danger was conjured for a long time.

We draw from this paradigmatic case some teachings. First, the people of higher culture felt threatened, on the verge of destruction, of what we have on record in the historians of the time. On the other hand, this situation was caused by the culture itself, whose irradiation had facilitated the peoples allochthonous the military means with which it was seriously threatened. And finally, the harassed society, knew how to draw forces of weakness, solving the problem, for which it was necessary that its structure be radically modified. We see in action one of those destructive germs that civilization carries with it, this time through external factors. The problem that concerns us now is of a very different contexture. They are not external factors, raised by civilization, that threaten it, but anomalous phenomena generated within it, which must be resolved. Greco-Latin society went through great danger and managed to overcome it, but the result could have been different.

The invasions could have succeeded at that time and ancient history would have been very different.

THE GREAT WALL

OF CHINA

In Mediterranean and Middle Eastern civilizations these situations intermittently ensued. But Chinese society has been under constant pressure for thousands of years. This was because in that territory there is a sudden transition from the regions where agriculture is possible to those in which it is practically impossible and had to be abandoned to the pastoral peoples. Chinese society is the most sedentary of all and instead of merging with nomadic desert populations, It has been isolated from they.

Only in the great eras of fullness, is the Chinese state expanded beyond the limits of working lands, seeking through large trade routes, such as Silk, a communication with the distant countries of the West. To achieve this defensive isolation they built a wall of 3,000 kilometres, which follows exactly the line that separates the crops from the pastures and joins the Yellow Sea with Tibet. It was both defensive wall and communications line, because on it runs a road. The Chinese gave this strange solution to their biggest problem.

Historians have often wondered about the reasons for such unusual fortification, since they were really unable to stop the passage of a moderately armed army. However, this wall was very useful. The Chinese did not take the course of a river - the Huang Ho - as a defensive line, as the Romans did against the Germans, but this line that separated farmers from shepherds. Throughout it they established a powerful defensive device, based on the settlers who populated the territories covered by the wall.

In the face of major military invasions, this device was insufficient, but not so in the face of the chronic danger caused by the neighborhood of Mongolian transhumant shepherds on the other side of the border. The presence of the huge wall, climbing mountains and saving chasms, was of great psychological and military effect. Only the great invasions could cross it, but the Chinese countryside was covered by the annual depredations against which nothing could be done, since the Chinese people would have had to adopt the way of life of the nomads to overcome them

The Chinese stubbornly resisted this change and

they preferred the solution to isolate themselves from them.

But the effect of this enormous engineering effort was that Chinese society was shaken from the feeling of anguish, of imminent danger, with which society cannot exist and develop. Chinese society could not go on as long as this sword of Damocles hung over it, which could destroy everything at any moment. We find here a paradigmatic example of what is intended to be presented in this analysis.

A civilization cannot develop under the risk that everything that is built with the collective effort is at risk of being destroyed at any time for whatever reason. You need to have the future open, that your effort has continuity. Time has to play in your favor. This is the situation in which we are today and of which the previous examples are a good example. The Chinese were faced with a tremendous problem and solved it in their own way. Thanks to the Great Wall, Chinese society did not live in anguish and terror and could give itself the splendid fruits of its millenary culture. He was not covered by the great military invasions, which coincided with his periods of crisis but with the constant and distressing pressure of a chronic threat.

SOCIABILITY

AND BELIGERANCE

We must consider the phenomenon of war, if we want to move on. It is a fact that is there, we like it or it disgusts us. War exists and is as old as man. We are not going to justify or disqualify it, since it is a phenomenon that is by itself, without the need for our approval and without our simple repulsion is enough to cancel it. While there are weapons or the technical capacity to manufacture them, there will be those who are willing to use them to obtain their purposes, cynical or sacrosanct.

The society is a coexistence of individuals, each of which exists since itself, as a separate world, individuals do not integrate into social life in an absolute and unconditional manner; They do not give up their individuality completely. On the contrary, they try to defend and preserve it. Hence, sociability and belligerence are two complementary factors without which society would not be possible. If the individual could not sustain a belligerence that defends his individuality, he would not be integrated into social life, into the collective. In social life there must be a balance between intimacy and community, between individualism and gregarious spirit. Let us observe, for example, that the greater the social pressure on individuals, the stronger the individualistic feeling. The most gregarious societies are those that, by reaction and need to defend themselves against it, more jealous people of their individual independence. The organizations that form certain animals called social are very different from human society. The individuals who form them do not fight each other, they do not try to differentiate themselves, since their individuality is the community.

Human society exists on condition that belligerence, defense of individuality exists. Without this condition, the individual would never have been integrated into social life and would never have overcome his organization the form of the family horde, sustained by the primitive forces of the blood instinct, of physiological affinity, as in animals.

War is nothing more than a manifestation, a form among others, of this radical belligerence that constitutes human society. But, in turn, in the face of inevitable belligerence, the complementary factor, the sociability, act with full force, counteracting and limiting it.

If belligerence is necessary for individualism to remain and man can be integrated into society, sociability should not be violated by this chronic belligerence. Society exists when these two factors are complementary and not antagonistic; when they face each other, society dissolves.

Each State forms a social individuality, against which are the remaining state individualities. Between states, cultural, idiomatic differences, economic, interest disputes, accentuate this individuality, separating and facing to each other. Each state unit forms a separate world, a different point of view, a different conception of problems. The phenomenon of radical belligerence, which attempts to defend the identity or individuality of state units, manifests itself in endless frictions, rivalries, disputes. The State is not the only social unit, the only area of coexistence of individuals, but it is the main one of them, because only he has collective material means, a body, physical limits.

War is but the extreme that adopts that belligerence, because through it a state unit intends to destroy another state unit.

Wars between states are the most frequent case in history. Much less frequent are the wars between social clans (revolutions and counterrevolutions) or wars between parts of the State (civil wars), when it is split and polarized into two antagonistic units.

This phenomenon is general, chronic, eviternity. But the elemental belligerence that constitutes one of the determining factors of social life does not necessarily have to manifest itself in the form of war. On the contrary, healthy rivalry, inevitable friction, should not degenerate into bitter disputes and irreversible, that lead to that dramatic situation in which survival of the social unit depends on the annihilation of another.

However, this is often the case. There we have the chronicle of the story, full of truculent struggles. To avoid it, it is necessary that the sociability, the spirit of coexistence, of concord, act with full force, looking for some natural conditions within which social peace can be restored. It is the antithesis between politics and war. It has been cynically said that politics is nothing more than the continuation of war, but by other means. This collective effort of a unit state to destroy another is one of the most dramatic and extreme phenomena that occur in social life and we often observe that, analysing the events, the war phenomenon could have been avoided, repressed, reduced to the lower tension that are the mere discrepancies .

WAR IN THE PEACE

The problem we face today is not that chronic belligerence, which sometimes manifests itself in the form of war, nor those appearances of militarism, the product of hypertrophied nationalism. The outbreak of the conflagration in our time is very difficult because of the existence of radioactive weapons. This is one of the virtues attributed to them, since it is said that the fear of nuclear destruction makes war impossible. We will see later what is true in this. What is evident is that nuclear weapons originate a new and unusual situation. In our time there are no extreme social causes or exacerbated nationalist rivalries, such as those of the first half of this century, that raise the tension between the states until they are on the brink of war. Most of the conflicts that exist today could be resolved peacefully. They are social, economic, cultural problems. They can be solved with the application of material means and with a general will of concord; Both things exist in today's   world.

However, despite the fact that the reasons for serious friction do not exist, in our time we are witnessing a wild and frantic arms race. For more than thirty years the great military powers have sustained it, trying to place themselves at a level of virtual superiority in the face of any conflagration that could explode in the indeterminate future. It is the fear of atomic weapons itself, of its tremendous capacity for extermination and annihilation, that generates this process of rising belligerence. We are today in a situation of larval, overlapping war.

The great powers -and, to their influence, all the others- they make disproportionate military expenses. There is, as in war, a constant wear of weapons, not because they are used, but because they have to be discarded before the appearance of more perfected ones. Its aftermath only manifests itself - later we will see how - in the economic and social field, by forcing society to make higher expenses than it can bear.

The arms race is not really a novelty. The struggle between the States of all ages has led to it. But to the arms race that we could call usual, with conventional weapons, adds at this time that some powers maintain with the manufacture of nuclear devices. To the traditional expenses of that, the exceptional ones of this one are added. However, the mutual fear of the possibility that these terrifying weapons are used by someone means that this struggle cannot be stopped. The social and economic problems of our time go to the background. They cannot be faced, since the resources that would be needed for this are destined to something that appears much more peremptory and unavoidable: preserve survival.

THE WAR EXPENSES IN THE GENERAL ECONOMY

The amount of military expenses that a State can make is very limited with respect to its economy as a whole. These are expenses that do not generate wealth directly or indirectly and, from a strictly economic point of view, are burdensome. Conceived the armies as an instrument of defense of the nation only produce a remote economic benefit, by dissuading other States from the possibility of violating their economy by coercive means. This is considered very important for the survival of the States and to that extent the economic effort that society makes for the maintenance of a military device it is seen as necessary. But the investments made in the military field do not generate wealth, they are not the origin of a production cycle. Hence, unlike the economic activities themselves, they do not support themselves, they do not generate new economic activity. For this reason, since economically military activity does not support itself, but must be borne by the rest of the economy, its development can only arise from the benefits of the general economy of a society.

These benefits, this economic surplus is very limited, represents a small percentage over the whole production.

Among state expenditures, the military is not the only ones that do not generate new wealth. Also a good part of those who serve to maintain social organization have that character. Only in the long term do they produce an economic benefit for society. The modern organization of society means that there is a state economy in many countries, whose investments produce an immediate economic improvement. Much of the social expenses are of this nature, as they contribute to the generation of wealth that strictly promote economic investments.

But only military expenses and expenses that maintain the social or administrative organization are, from a purely economic point of view, a burden on society, which faces them for the reasons outlined above to maintain social organization and ensure survival.

Hence, society must be very prudent with these types of expenses that do not contribute to generating new economic activities immediately. If hypertrophy occurs, the economy runs the risk of suffocation. The economic potential of a country and its ability to sustain unlimited war effort.

Even in a state of war, only part of the productive capacity can be dedicated to its maintenance. If military spending exceeds a certain limit, the economy is in serious danger, and this is the situation it seems to have reached today. When state and military expenses go beyond bearable, they become parasites that ruin society. If expenses considered necessary, they become simply parasitic. The double arms race, which increases the economic effort, is the cause.

MILITARISM

When this happens, we are at the threshold of a new situation. If military expenses do not exceed a certain limit, society can bear them without trauma. But if they go further, the phenomenon occurs that, in order not to be unbearable to the society that makes them, they are tried to become a source of income that compensates for the excessive expenses incurred and makes them bearable. The military function, conceived as something defensive, can become predatory and give rise to one of the forms of militarism. War becomes the source of income which covers military expenses that society cannot sustain itself. The hypertrophy of military expenses leads inexorably to war, because only through the war of conquest can society cope with them.

The paradoxical phenomenon then occurs that, considering armies as instruments to avoid war, when this economic limit is exceeded, they become a cause of war, since only they can continue to exist. This gives rise to the most serious and dangerous form of militarism.

There is a militarism that is born of excessive nationalism; In it, one nation only sees itself and ignores and belittles the power of others. Driven by his stupidity, he embarks on grim, foolish military adventures. A recent case is found in Germany half a century ago, that "a priori" could not win the war and, nevertheless, tried, with the known result.

But there is a much more serious militarism that appears when the military function is excessive for the economic power that sustains it and then war arises as a necessity, which is precise, through it, to compensate with the pillage the expenses that are realized with the maintenance of an excessive military device and that the society cannot face. This disproportionate military device needs war to continue existing. There are many examples of this in history, but perhaps the most notable is that of the Assyrians, who in the late 10th century BC maintained a state organization that lived on war and for war, systematically devastating the countries of West Asia and nourishing these depredations, until

they were destroyed by yet more
extreme militarism.

ARMAMENTISM

Numerous factors that once strongly conditioned war activity have lost their value in our time. Armament is today the only important war factor. The technical innovations that are carried out in this field have a much greater significance than they had in the past, although the innovations have been constant throughout history. The strictly armamentism event takes on our special time. Before that factor was decisive, but it was conditioned by others, especially obstacles that Nature imposes on the war activity. Within the current situation only the power of weapons comes into play. It is a rare and unusual situation, which has only happened between small and very close states. In this sense, the current war is a bell war, like the internal struggles between factions of the Italian medieval cities, which from their high towers were harassed by a crossbow shot. However, the resemblance ends here, because in the face of the offensive and destructive power there is no defensive power than the counter.

We are not yet immersed in the problem of militarism, which occurs when a State is willing to use its military means in a conscious manner and without circumstances having put it in the trigger. Today we are faced with the problem of armamentism, which occurs when there is the anomalous situation that only the weapons count. It is pure armamentism, without tactics, without strategy; Only quantity, power and scope of explosive devices.

THE ECONOMIC FIGHT IN THE ARMAMENTS RACE

Developing the current war struggle mainly in the form of an arms race, the industrial capacity to manufacture them is the only decisive factor. It is definitely the economic factors that determine which is the winner. But there is a notable misunderstanding in this matter. Western countries have considerable financial superiority over those of the eastern bloc, if one considers their economic production as a whole. But the economy of the countries of the East, having state production methods in which there are no intermediaries,   perform the manufacture of these warlike devices at a lower cost. On the other hand, if Western economies have a larger global production because their economy is much more diversified and heterogeneous, in the basic productions that supply the elements with which nuclear and conventional weapons are manufactured, Eastern economies are not inferior. Westerners base their hopes of winning this arms production race on general statistical data, not on the specific data that matters.

In this area, equality is remarkable.

This nuclear engineering manufacturing career cannot be won by anyone and prolong it further is a foolishness that is already producing the first consequences today: the general impoverishment of the world that is beginning to be observed.

UNIVERSAL BELIGERANCE

The possibility of widespread destruction using atomic weapons causes a feeling of insecurity, a sense of collective danger that all states share. Instead of a climate of distension and trust, unconsciously reacts to this hypothetical danger, seeking how many militaries means their economies allow them and even those that they cannot afford. The conservation instinct of nations acts in this way. No one can feel safe, the danger is universal.

To this are added internal social conflicts, which cannot be resolved due to lack of material means and because there is no such security climate. We have repeatedly indicated that the economic means that would be necessary to solve social problems are largely destined to the arms race of the great powers. The State, unable to address its social and economic problems, is facing increasing internal difficulties that cannot be solved. The State feels in danger within the State, because society turns against it. State and society become antagonistic: a chasm opens between them.

The state organization reacts to the problem by taking a defensive attitude towards society, repressing social conflicts since it cannot solve them. The State thus increases its military means to protect itself from social reaction and the turbulence that accompanies it.

On the other hand, to this double process of increase of the military means of the States corresponds an increase of the border tensions, because the States have more warlike means than in fact, they need. This increased military capacity of one and the other is a danger to each and every one.

No State feels safe behind its borders, in the face of neighbors who have military means often superabundant. In this way, the general feeling of danger in the face of a universal conflagration and the increase in social conflicts, border tensions are added, as the states feel less and less safe from others. In our time, numerous border wars are taking place, born of the hypertrophy of military capacity and as a means of diverting social tensions abroad.

The arms race among the great powers has been accompanied for some years by an arms race in most of the remaining States, who feel insecure, threatened. This is a phenomenon as serious as that. The military effort that many countries with weak economies are making in our time goes beyond everything reasonable. Not all of them, but a good part of their social and economic problems would be solved if those arms costs were destined for this purpose. But it is not done because there is a collective feeling of distrust and because, in reality, their problems would not be completely solved either by applying those resources to give way to political and social problems- This solution cannot be a work exclusive to the minor states, each one in itself, but must come from a collective action of the international community, since only at that level can they be resolved.

BALANCE BETWEEN OFFENSIVE AND DEFENSIVE WEAPONS

There is also a very serious problem in our time: the balance between offensive and defensive weapons. It is not a specifically military issue, since its transcendence today is dramatic. Offensive weapons have always been at the forefront of innovations, since the purpose of the war, although it is said that the armies are to defend society, are conceived to overcome the resistance of alleged adversaries. For this reason, innovations in military technique they have always started with offensive, destructive weapons.

defences, capable of resisting the impact of others, have been created later. The appearance of a new offensive weapon has always posed a serious problem that has been attempted to solve and has not always been achieved.

During the First World War the masses of artillery fire were so excessive that, having nothing capable of resisting them, the deadly consequences are well known. In reaction to this, the first armoured vehicles appear, capable of counteracting them. The enormous power of artillery at the beginning of the century prompted the appearance of armoured vehicles.

During the Second World War, a certain balance is maintained between both types of weapons, but at the end of the day, atomic weapons of irresistible power and indelible contamination arise. Almost forty years have elapsed without the presence of other destructive weapons that have restored balance. The world is unarmed in the face of such colossal destructive power.

Military organizations have put great effort into developing and applying radioactive weapons, whose deadly capacity is unstoppable. But it has not given the slightest step to cancel its power through ingenuity or devices capable of resisting its impact. Only offensive weapons capable of intercepting the adversary's offensive weapons have been put into play; they are offensive weapons like the others that play the role of defensive. This interception could fail, and any target would be left unarmed.

But here we stumble upon the greatest and most terrible of problems, because in the face of these offensive weapons, there can be no defensive weapons. Its power is such that underground fortifications, hundreds or thousands of meters deep, autonomous, protected by rock masses, would be necessary in the that the impact didn't make a dent. The world would have to be filled with these troglodyte devices, the only guarantee that the attacker cannot completely destroy the means of response. Is this the future that awaits humanity? Meanwhile, radiation would have destroyed most of life on Earth and these enclaves would be their last refuge.

This is a decisive and incontestable reason for that type of armament to be abandoned in an absolute and radical way: there is no defense against it.

To the man is not interested in fighting with a weapon against which he has no defense if he is also in the hands of the adversary. This has been a general rule in history. Other weapons of exorbitant deadly efficacy have been in the hands of man and have not been used for that reason; Thus, the toxins that man could have always used because countless plants supply it and have been used in pharmacopoeia, in hunting, since time immemorial. However, this destructive method has not been used because it attacks life, not just the supposed opponent.

Poisoning water with toxic is

something that It could have been done very easily, but that toxicity remains perennial, ruining life and livelihoods.

Radioactive weapons are of this nature. The least is its tremendous explosive power. The vital annihilation that its radiation causes causes absolutely irreparable damage throughout existence. Only certain very primitive peoples, who live scattered and terrified, lost in the rainforests, today use chemical weapons equivalent to them. Radioactive weapons are, in short, nothing more than chemical weapons and the current civilization is giving samples of an inexplicable barbarism to match the indigenous people of the Amazon.

Man has suddenly discovered the enormous maelstrom of nuclear disintegration and seems to have lost the sense of reality. These are not weaponing that correspond to our time; Its destructive capacity is not a function of the military resistance to be overcome. They are spawners for another time, monsters that, by such, seem antediluvian. It is as if the Mesozoic monsters had returned   to Earth   and   tried   to reconquer she, destroying the life that exists today and restoring what was one hundred million years ago. This is the path that Humanity undoubtedly leads, if the most serious and peremptory of its problems is not resolved, whose solution cannot be other than the absolute and radical abandonment of these absurd and aberrant weapons.

RIVALRY BETWEEN NUCLEAR AND WEAPONS WITH BLINDAGE

Doubt is raised about the effectiveness of this type of weapons in the strictly military field. It is likely that a fight for the predominance between radioactive and armored weapons will be unleashed in the near future. These are two different forms of war, and even antagonistic, although they seem complementary. Radioactive weapons have their effectiveness against human targets - cities, production and communications systems -, dismantling and devastating the economic device of the adversary, at the cost of carrying out that terrible pollution to the that nothing escapes. It is a weapon that produces destructive effects on the economy, annihilating livelihoods. But what real effectiveness does this destructive form have against mechanized and armoured armies? These act in a scattered, mobile, autonomous way, without offering a defined target.

Undoubtedly, if this process is followed, parallel to the progress of nuclear weapons will be developed, that of mechanized armies, increasingly autonomous, less dependent on specific industrial centers, capable of acting with absolute independence from them, scattered enough so that the effectiveness of nuclear weapons is diluted. If there is no voluntary renunciation of the use of radioactive weapons, which are counterproductive and unnecessary, the world will be populated by large mechanized armies as a last guarantee against a nuclear attack. These armoured armies would evolve in the sense of becoming invulnerable to chemical or radioactive weapons and, perhaps, may continue to act after a attack nuclear in which the means of production of a country have been annihilated. It is the last alternative that will remain in the face of the superiority that in nuclear weapons some powers monopolize. The resistance of the people attacked with radioactive weapons would then focus on these conventional devices. On the road that leads, a struggle for world domination will take place between conventional armies and rocket ramps and satellites carrying nuclear weapons. The characters of this contest can be imagined. It is something that will end up happening, because mechanized armies will not yield supremacy.

If nuclear technology is available to many countries today, the same does not happen with its large-scale use, which depends on the contribution of radioactive minerals over whose production a jealous control is exercised. Only a limited number of countries will be able to manufacture them in large quantities and they will always have superiority in that field. On the contrary, the manufacture of armored weapons corresponds to a simpler and more widespread technology, which is available to a greater number of countries. Existing this antagonism between the two war modes, the countries threatened by the nuclear superiority of a few, they will try to preserve their survival through the development of increasingly autonomous armoured armies. This produces another multiplier effect, in which the growth of nuclear weapons caused a steady increase in armoured forces, which is accelerating in the world in recent years.

THE ARMED PEACE

Precisely one of the facts that make the possibility of a peace agreement between the great powers difficult, based on a military balance, is that if there is a certain equality in the field of nuclear weapons, the same thing does not seem to be the case. Conventional weapons: the Eastern military bloc seems to have a manifest superiority. It would take a balance in conventional weapons to make what is called "armed peace" possible. The huge mass of armoured block of the East, which in a few weeks could reach the Strait from Gibraltar or from Hormuz, they are one more factor to take into account than their launching ramps.

The use of these, in case of conflagration, falls within the hypothetical, may not occur, but the advancement of that machine is safe and irresistible.

Westerners try to counteract this superiority with the development of strategic weapons of doubtful effectiveness in the specifically military field. It is necessary that a balance be reached regarding conventional weapons so that peace is possible, and the use of radioactive weapons is discarded. If that balance is not achieved, this vital objective for human survival will be out of the possible.

It is within conventional weapons that equality must be achieved so that nuclear balance is not necessary and the use of these lethal devices is abandoned.

PRESSURE POLICY

The economic effort that the two great military powers make for the maintenance of the arms race is disproportionate with their own means. This translates into the huge deficit of its economy, in one case, and the inability to get out of the stalemate, in another. The consequences for the world economy are very serious, as all countries collaborate, directly or indirectly, in this struggle. The 800,000 million dollars spent last year on military budgets are more than just a figure: they are the expression of a dangerous state of affairs; it's much more than the economy world can stand.

But these expenses not only remain, but they increase and the cause is in the pressure policy that the great powers exert among themselves, thinking that it is the means to win the race, to place the adversary in inferior conditions.

However, this concept is based on a wrong assumption. A pressure can be exerted when there is superiority of one of the two parts. But not in this case, there being some equality. Through pressure it will not be reduced, to contain the opposite.

Even if there is not a remarkable superiority, this pressure policy always gives the expected results. An example of this is the recent confrontation between the United States and Japan in the Pacific half a century ago. The American industrial power was ten times higher than the Japanese. The Japanese territories were surrounded by a formidable military device that it was thought that the Japanese were going to resign. This would have been the case if the Japanese had the pragmatic spirit of the Americans, but their mentality is very different and, with it, their reaction to this policy of pressure.

The result is known: a desperate reaction.

It is precisely these desperate reactions that we must prevent, because they are not out of the question today. If the deterioration of the economy, accentuated by general impoverishment, reaches a point that cannot be found out, in a few years it will be possible that a senseless reaction will take place by one of the parties. Indeed, if a reasonable solution is not seen, irrational solutions will come into play. Then the possibility of a hand strike, an attack by surprise - one of those infallible plans that there are always who they happen to him-, whose results would be, with all possibility the catastrophe of all Humanity. It is a possibility that is there, it is a risk that we run. Achieving a solid military balance, based on weapons that cannot produce these annihilating consequences, is the only solution.

EPILOGUE

The current man is playing nonsense. Nobody wants a war of this nature to happen and, deep down, nobody believes it can break out. But it is pretended to be believed and acted as if it were believed. In fact, it is acting as if apocalyptic destruction, by the hand of man, was possible and the means are put for it. It is the old fable of the shepherd and the wolf. Because that hypothetical wolf that is threatened and not expected to appear, could poke his ears the day less thought. The facts may become stronger than the wills and it is It is necessary to prevent from now on a situation that seems inevitable with the evolution of events.

For this it is necessary:

1st. Absolutely renounce the use of radioactive weapons, leaving only conventional weapons in operation. If a balance is reached in this area, lasting peace can be achieved. In the worst case, conventional weaponry is more than enough to settle any power dispute.

2nd. Create social and political conditions so that these war conflicts, even with conventional weapons, do not have to explode. If you stop making the huge expenditure on nuclear weapons and these resources will be dedicated to the material solution of social problems, within an atmosphere of relaxation and trust, we would have the basis for war conflicts to be out of place.

Our era needs to solve this problem. The use of nuclear weapons means, neither more nor less, the beginning of the end of the world. Will it be necessary for a genocidal catastrophe to occur for humanity to survive fiercely?

SYNOPSIS

We are today in a situation of larval, overlapping war. The great powers - and, to their influence, all the others - make disproportionate military expenses. There is, as in war, a constant wear of weapons, not because they are used, but because they must be discarded before the appearance of more perfected ones. Its aftermath only manifests itself - later we will see how - in the economic and social field, by forcing society to make higher expenses than it can bear.

The arms race is not really a novelty. The struggle between the States of all ages has led to it.

Man has suddenly discovered the enormous maelstrom of nuclear disintegration and seems to have lost the sense of reality. These are not weapons that correspond to our time; Its destructive capacity is not a function of the military resistance to be overcome. They are spawners for another time, monsters that, by such, seem antediluvian. It is as if the Mesozoic monsters had returned to Earth and tried to reconquer she destroying the life that exists today and restoring what was one hundred million years ago.

This is the path that Humanity undoubtedly leads, if the most serious and peremptory of its problems is not resolved, whose solution cannot be other than the absolute and radical abandonment of these absurd and aberrant weapons.

BIOGRAPHY

Self-taught, Juan Sanz Sanz (1943-2019), devoted himself, from early youth, to unravelling the problems posed by the readings of historical events narrated by the various authors who frequently diverged from each other.

Geography was one of his great hobbies and reason for fervent study, not existing on the planet place, no matter how remote it was, that had not been fully informed.

The attentive follow-up of the social and political reality in which its existence took place resulted in proposals for water use on three continents and each of the projects was sent in its day to the places that were most suitable for its achievement.

Languages - French, English, Italian, Portuguese and German, in addition to his own, Spanish - had no secrets for him and thus he could fully enjoy the literature written on them, another hobby in which, as an enlightened man, he found his peers.

In early youth the Spanish guitar and later the piano, were musical instruments to which he dedicated a great effort similar to the passion that the music awoke in him and thus, in maturity, with authentic devotion and delicacy, he interpreted beautiful pieces of Bach, Chopin, Debussy and Beethoven who contributed a lot to make their days more human and the passage of time milder.

In addition to the Water Projects, it leaves many literary works almost ready to publish, something that will be sought in the public light.

Amazon´s Page of author:

Amazon.com/author/juansanzsanz